The merry-go-round

Story by Jenny Giles
Illustrations by Meredith Thomas

"Look, Ben," said Kate.

"I can see a merry-go-round."

"A merry-go-round," said Ben.
"I like the duck."

"I'm going on the horse,"
said Kate.

Mom said,

"You can go on the merry-go-round.
I will stay here."

"Come on, Ben," said Kate.

"Oh, no!" said Ben.

"I can not go on the duck."

"And I can not go on the horse," said Kate.

"Look," said Ben.
"I can see a car!"

"You can go in the car,"
said Kate.
"I will stay here."

"Come here, Kate," said Ben.
"This is a **big** car.
You can come in, too."

"I like this car," said Kate.

"This is a **good** car,"
said Ben.

Kate and Ben

went on the merry-go-round.